Bison

Edel Wignell

CELEBRATION PRESS
Pearson Learning Group

Map of the World

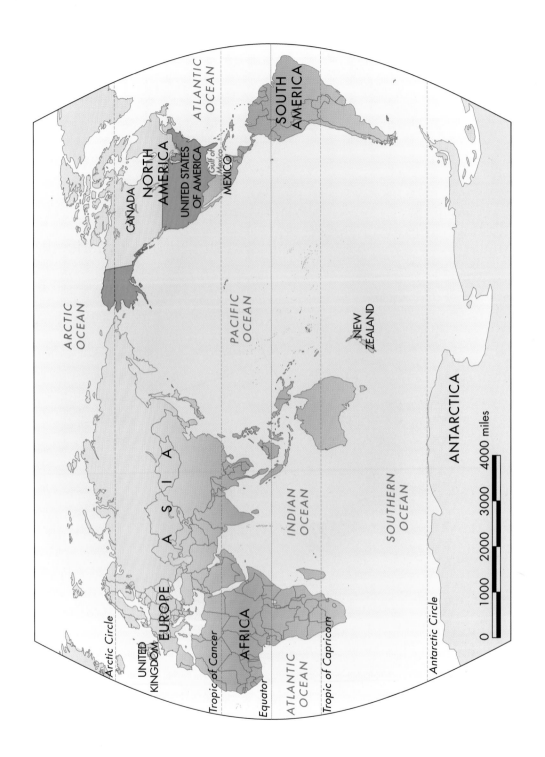

Contents

What Are Bison?

The American bison is a large, hump-backed animal with short, curved horns and a long tail. It has a thick and shaggy, dark brown coat.

The bison is North America's largest land mammal. It can stand at 6 and one-half feet in height and can be 12 and one-half feet long. It can weigh 2,000 pounds.

Bison eat prairie grasses and plants. If necessary, they will also eat leaves from trees.

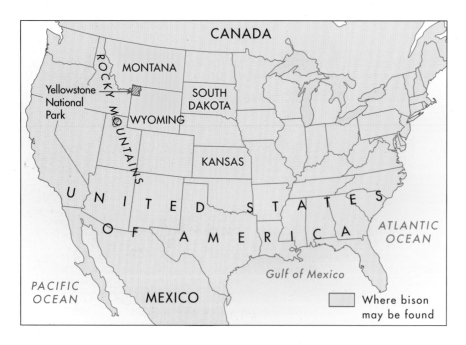

Where bison may be found in the United States

Bison are also called plains buffalo, American buffalo, and American bison.

The Bison Family

Bison are wild animals that are in the same family as sheep, goats, and cattle.

Close relatives of the American bison are the Canadian wood bison and the European bison, also called *wisent*.

The wood bison is the largest land mammal in Canada. It can stand at 6 feet in height and be 12 and one-half feet long. It can weigh up to 2,200 pounds. At one time, wood bison were hunted almost to extinction. There are only about 2,300 of these animals left in the wild.

Canadian wood bison

The European bison is the largest land mammal in Europe. It can stand over 6 feet tall and can be 9 and one-half feet long. It can weigh up to 2,200 pounds. The largest population of European bison live in a national park located in an ancient forest in Poland. There are only about 3,200 of these animals left.

European bison

American bison

Where the Bison Roamed

At one time, there were millions of bison living in North America, from Canada to Mexico. They roamed the prairies and the mountains.

No one knows exactly how many bison there once were. There may have been as many as 60 million.

The Great Plains of North America
are called prairies. These large areas
of grassland are home to bison.

Bison and the Native Americans

The Native Americans were the first people to live in North America. Traditionally, Native Americans live in different nations or tribes. Each nation has its own name and territory.

In the past, many Native Americans depended on the bison. They often used bows and arrows for hunting. They killed only a few bison—just enough to meet their needs. They did not have horses until European people arrived.

After European people arrived, the Native Americans had horses and guns.

The Native Americans of North America lived with the bison for thousands of years. Bison were part of their culture and tradition. They needed these animals for food, shelter, clothing, and tools. They used every part of the bison in their everyday lives. Nothing was wasted.

Traditional Uses of the Bison

• hide	containers, ropes, moccasins, drums, saddles, cradles, winter robes, bedding, shirts, bags
• horns	arrowheads, cups, spoons, toys, medicine
• hair	headdresses, pillows, ropes, bracelets
• hoofs and feet	glue, rattles, spoons
• teeth	decorations, ornaments
• bones	pipes, shovels, plates, knives, forks
• flesh	fresh meat, sausages, dried food
• muscles	bows, thread
• fat	soaps, hair grease, cosmetics
• blood	soups, puddings, paints
• chips	waste used for fire fuel
• tail	fly swatters, whips

Hunting the Bison

Europeans arrived in North America long ago. First, they hunted beavers for the fur trade. When they saw the bison, they knew its hide could be sold. Bison were also killed for sport.

Two parts of the bison were valuable—the robe and the tongue. Bison robes were used by Europeans as gowns or rugs. Bison tongues and the meat were used as food.

These bison products were sent in great wagonloads across the country to the East coast. Soon, bones also were sent. These bones were ground up for use as fertilizer.

For many, many years, the bison hunters killed thousands of animals every year.

Bison hides ready to be taken across the country to the East coast.

Near-Extermination of the Bison

When railroads were built, more and more bison products were sent away. By the 1880s, there were very few bison left. They were nearly extinct.

People who cared about animals were worried. They could see that the bison was in danger of extinction. By 1884, there were only about 300 bison left.

With the arrival of European settlers, ruthless hunting of the bison began. Between 1830 and 1860, the killing increased.

Saving the Bison

In 1905, the American Bison Society was formed. It persuaded the U.S. government to create wildlife reserves to protect this endangered animal. With the help of bison owners, protection of the bison began.

In 1919, there were 12,521 bison. In 1929, a total of 3,385 bison were counted. Now the bison count is at about 250,000. Some herds are privately owned, and some are in public parks.

The largest public bison herd is in Yellowstone National Park in the state of Wyoming. There are over 4,000 bison in the park. Anyone can visit the park and see these magnificent animals grazing safely.

Glossary

ancient	very old
culture	a way of living
endangered	in danger of dying off
exterminated	killing or destroying completely
extinct	having died out
fertilizer	substance that helps plants grow
herds	large groups of animals, such as bison
hide	skin of an animal
Native Americans	the indigenous people of the Americas
near-extermination	almost exterminated
population	total number of people or animals living in a place
reserves	land set aside for a special purpose
robes	cleaned and prepared bison hides
ruthless	without pity
shaggy	with long, rough hair
sport	as a game
tradition	very old habit or practice
tribes	groups of families living together in a traditional way
valuable	worth a lot of money